Poured Out

Poured Out

POEMS BY
KEELEY BRUNER

Thea Press

Poured Out
by Keeley Bruner

Thea Press
P.O. Box 24905
Tempe, AZ 85285
www.theapress.org

Cover art by Jason Bruner.

Cover design by Andrea Dobbins and Megan Hall.

ISBN-13: 978-1-956604-11-5 (Paperback)

These poems are dedicated
to the maidens, mothers, and crones
who helped bring them forth
as their creative midwives,
and to Jason,
the best partner I could imagine

Delicate Threads

Sarah moves around the circle holding the thread,
tenderly circling each of our wrists,
one, two, three loops
binding us to create a web of womanhood,
of motherhood,
of sisterhood
we read poetry extolling the blood and milk of our bodies,
praising the beauty and power
we are woven together: maiden, mother, and crone

my belly is swollen,
full of my son who will be born in the coming weeks
the women surround me,
enfolding and empowering me with sacredness and
intimacy

his young sisters among them,
they place hands on me,
feeling my fullness,
offering benedictions of joy and peace, harmony and
courage,
marveling at the miracle.

Postpartum: Through a Glass Darkly

It's oddly symmetrical,
the tears rolling down my cheek onto my pillow
Mirroring my healing womb,
bleeding slowly but relentlessly
My left breast,
weeping in sympathy
as the baby gently pulses on its mate
All of this pouring out of myself
This involuntary deflating of all my parts
This is my body, my blood, poured out for whom?

My mind remains apart,
unyielding
Standing with its arms crossed, interrogating:
"What have you got to be sad about?"
Accusing:
"Isn't this what you wanted?"
Pressing:
"Why are you complaining when you have so much to
be grateful for?"
And my poor body,
my fragile soul,
reply in weak defense:
Yes, but, can one not be grateful, and exhausted?

I rub my face,
seeking
almost desperate
against the newborn head,
covered in downy fuzz
I breathe deep
of the milky, sweet scalp
and pray for sleep

6am Shift Change: Daddy's Turn

Squishy foam torpedoes
fill my ears
expanding slowly
flooding my mind with blissful
semi-silence
farther
into an ocean
of soundlessness
my pulsing heartbeat a tide
to drown out the sweet symphony
of cooing, babbling beauty:

my firstborn.
I float in dreamless sleep
as she swims
in other arms.

Lesson

You're doing all the right things, Baby,
I say,
gently patting his back
as I cradle him
on my shoulder
after a 2am feeding

He settles quickly
into the heavy, shallow breathing
of newborn sleep
as his eyelids flicker

Finding a rhythm
punctuated
by soft squeaks and snores
his body molds to my chest
as he relaxes
into the work
of forming synapses

His mouth forms
a fleeting smile
in the dim light
saying,
I know
watch and learn

Practice

I remember practicing
on my violin
a small passage in
The Reformation Symphony
while at summer music camp
an arpeggiated pattern
complicated to my adolescent fingers
over and over and over
I can hum it in my head to this day

It comes to mind as I reflect
on watching a new mama
learn to feed her baby
the football hold
baby latches
and releases
the cross-cradle hold
baby suckles
mama grimaces
that's not the latch
the cradle hold
until finally, baby is swallowing
and mama closes her eyes
and relaxes for a moment

I witness
I observe
I say, "You're doing everything right"
and "It takes time"
and "It's very common to need practice to figure
it out"
I remember my own scars
how long it took my first baby and me to learn
as she slowly grew

I come back the next week
baby has grown three ounces
it takes three seconds to latch
and *The Reformation Symphony*
echoes in my mind

Mommy Brain

Tell me about mommy brain
when you have figured out
all the parts of a breast pump
and how to fit it properly,
clean it,
store the milk,
and use it to keep a human alive
with your own body

Tell me about mommy brain
when you understand
all the components and mechanics
of the slow-flo bottles,
baby carriers,
wraps–woven and stretchy–
car seats,
and strollers
that help define
our new existence

Tell me about mommy brain
when you begin to differentiate among
all the cries your baby makes,
whether they are hungry,
sleepy,
lonely,
or gassy
or in what combinations

Tell me about mommy brain
when you have learned
14 different ways to soothe your baby,
depending on the time of day,
where you are,
and what tools you have available

I say learn
because none of us
were born knowing this,
just as we were not born
knowing calculus or parts of speech.
We learned it,
but unlike those other things
there is no textbook,
and the places you look for answers
vary vastly in their advice

So when you have figured out
how one can make room in their body
in their mind
and in their soul
for this new life
and not lose sight
of their very self
we will talk about mommy brain
in hushed tones of reverence,
marveling at
this holy transformation,
humbled by its power.

Witnessing Magic

learning to discover
to hone and honor
that latent instinct
which makes it feel
as though you've been stroking
your baby's hair for years
during the first week of life

learning to be patient
to give yourself space
and grace
growing from miscues
rather than succumbing
to that ever-tempting
feeling of failure

learning to lean into creativity
knowing that the world
is ever changing
is not what your ancestors knew
and is not what your baby will know
you navigate
the here and now

I say, "You are doing it right"
and your brows relax
your shoulders visibly soften
I say, "You are learning so much
and listening to your baby so well"
and your face lights up
swallowed in a smile

learning to trust the ancient wisdom
hard-won through the millennia
we have been alive
yet ever adapting to where we find ourselves
your body is magic
your blood is magic
your touch is magic
you are magic

Last Night as I Slept

Last night as I slept
I sifted through a ragged bag of clothes.
My fingers recognized
the linen of the skirt
I was wearing the day I met you,
the worn cotton of the dress
I wore on our first date.

"You look beautiful," you had said.

Deeper into the bag
I found my favorite pair of slacks,
the ones that grew with me
through seven years
of your graduate programs,
and my beloved pinstripe blouse—
pilfered from my mother's closet,
her initials on the pocket.

Through gauzy maternity tops
and nursing shirts I meandered,
remembering days of expectation and bliss.
I am at once maiden, bride, breadwinner, and mother,
a multifaceted identity
of fabric and dream.

Buttons

You fidget as my fingers fumble
with the tiny lavender buttons
of your second birthday dress

Your soft, pink, chubby back
squeezed into the cotton,
your strawberry blond ponytail bouncing
as you stand on one foot, then the other

I imagine these buttons in other iterations:
a zipper for a formal ensemble,
a theater costume,
a wedding sheath,
a doctoral hood,
a hospital gown tie

May you fit in time,
and find your style,
knowing my support
for whatever garments you choose.

And, please accept my thanks
for your help
with some of my own.

Pretty Free

There's no place freer
than a room full of preschool girls
working on crafts
they bend and stretch
for markers and paint
reaching for glue and glitter,
hopping across the room for play dough
when a different inspiration strikes

Elastic leggings ride down
and shirts ride up
tutus bounce
and bejeweled sandals prance
mismatched socks slouch
and lopsided ponytails sag
their bodies move
oblivious to appearance

"I like your picture!"
followed by an attempt to copy it
or maybe not
wherever the spirit leads
smiles and nods
of appreciation
fill the space

Everyone is pretty
all the work is pretty
we are all pretty
and there is enough pretty
to go around

First Day of School

This morning we experienced our first hustle and bustle of
        Kindergarten drop-off,
all hairbows and water bottles and tearful goodbyes.
Tiny bodies weighed down by superfluous backpacks,
a mass of arms and legs stretching for the safety of parents
and the adventure of new friends.

Hugs upon hugs and kisses upon kisses,
we finally separated, the turning point when I mentioned
the smell of French Toast.
Oh yes, the tide turned when you realized
maple syrup was in your future.

Courageously, but not without trepidation
you grabbed your friend's hand.
And as though preparing to enter Narnia,
you ventured, "Want to go together?"

Waving enthusiastically, blowing kisses,
and grinning beatifically at your little sister
you turned and entered that new land,
being careful to assure us that "we would be okay."

And so through an unexpectedly quiet bowl of yogurt and
        blueberries,
and a subdued morning of reading to your sister
I wondered how the French Toast went down.
As I put your sister down for her nap
and began my own period of rest and writing,
I considered the chicken tenders on the lunch menu
and how much of them remained on your plate.
I wished to text you and see
how your five-year-old body and mind were holding up
without us through the afternoon.

This day doesn't feel as though it's come too fast.
I have been present, through teething and stomach bugs,
through hundreds of books read and songs sung,
puzzles worked and dolls dressed, naps taken and meals
        eaten.
You have grown, indeed,
and I have been paying attention, my friend.
And we will still live our lives together,
but this changes things, doesn't it?
Just another step in your journey, Darling,
of being less of me and more of you.

Last First Day

Yesterday I nursed you to sleep
and you napped
curled next to my body
your head on my arm

We have spent the last three years
and three months
within arm's reach of each other
save six days
–thanks to grandparents–
and maybe a couple hours
here and there
your childhood rhythms impacted
by a global pandemic
in ways I could never have known
or expected

Today you began preschool
with your Dr. Seuss bag over your arm
ball cap on your head
potty reminder watch on your wrist
cowboy boots on your feet
slathered in sunscreen
and I have written emails with no distraction
besides the internal 30-minute alarm
to tell you to use the potty
I have done laundry
with no "help" hanging the swimsuits
on the drying rack
I watched the dump truck pick up the recycling
knowing I will now be the only one to applaud his efforts
I will prepare lunch for myself only
and will not eat it while watching
The Lion King

And I will not feel sorry–
I will not lament anything
or feel that this moment has come too soon
I have been here,
and you have been here,
and we will all still be here
with more to bring to the table
having gathered experiences apart from each other
and honestly,
I can't wait to hear about your day.

Littlest Mama

The littlest Mama in our house
has green eyes, grey fur,
and a purr you can hear across the room.

As a kitten she talked a big game,
routinely jumping feet in the air after a bird feather toy
only to hide under the bed
when a bluejay once came in through the stove vent.

Skittish and wary,
few visitors could charm her
and she has taught us
over nearly fifteen years
the best ways to show our love–
blinking thoughtfully
while smiling slightly
and following very, very careful petting patterns
of very, very specific parts
at very, very specific times
(depending on her mood)

But she is one of only three living creatures present
at the births of all three of our children,
and began her career as a mother
by meowing to alert us to our daughter's cries
and keeping watch by her cradle

She still observes our growing brood
with love and attention,
if not outright interaction.
She keeps a watchful eye
and rests easy when everyone gets
the snuggles they need.

Goldilocks

My family used to tease me
for collecting "families" of household items:
my baby garden trowel
ranging up to
our largest "Grandaddy-sized" flat shovel;
the screwdriver family,
each of my own family members represented
in the range of variation;
even the soap family arranged in order
of how much they'd each worn down.

I never tired of visiting Bojangles,
with their tiny windows
which my family knew as "Keeley-sized."

Now I consider our brood of three:
(small, medium, large)
and like Goldilocks in her quest,
it feels just right.

Friends

You are not a football hero
and I am not a supermodel
you are not a rock star
and I am not a famous CEO

We are not billionaires
with vacation homes
in London
Paris
and Honolulu
having to decide how
to spend our money
or ever see each other
face to face

Instead we sit at our table
and luxuriate
in eggs, toast, and tea
we catch each other up
on our latest frivolities
you show me what you carved
I show you what I wrote
you tell me about your drawing
I play you a new song
we budget for the car payment
and wonder when we will finally pay it off

We are not shiny
we are not lithe and supple
in short, our elastic is shot
But we have stretched and grown
together
and, wouldn't you know,
we still fit.

Southwest Journey

Towering rock formations in shades
of red, beige, and purple
rise into the sky like sandcastles
You muse,
"I wonder what it would be like
to get down there,"
and the next day we climb
on goblins of red rock,
finding our way
to the tops of the highest domes
giving each other hands up
and pushes from behind
the only proof a photo
in which we are so small
as to be invisible

Each day you reach for my hands—
one, two, three of you
one prefers to hold a pinkie finger,
one prefers to be on the left side
one peppers us
with endless questions and observations
And I bumble,
"Oh man, guys, look at that!
What do you think?"
at a loss for coherent words
in the face of this wonder

We visit the homeplaces
of long ago inhabitants

Wupatki, Ute, Paiute
who tamed the dry cliffs
carving their homes from sandstone
and using every drop of the scant water
We marvel at the resourcefulness
and begin to learn
that even as we are separated
by time and circumstance
we are alike,
delighting in the cold air blowing up
from an underground spring
and the acoustics of a ball court

Soil made of lava,
flowers growing up through
what looks like asphalt,
pine trees crying tears of sap–
scenting the air and staining our car–
multilevel rock fins
which become windows and arches,
a half moon out my cabin window,
the Big Dipper bright in the clear sky
an idyllic picnic in the oasis of Fruita
the awe on your faces,
sifting sand through your fingers,
climbing onto tall boulders
to stand with arms outstretched,
beholding the views
from the rim trails and overlooks,
resonating in your souls
with the cosmos surrounding you
your hearts beating

to ancient rhythms
of earth, water, and wind

The magic in these beautiful moments
is weaving our collective life,
that bank of memory and identity
which will be there for you–always.

Other Worlds

It amazes me how much mindspace
you can give to *Harry Potter*
dressing your Ron and Hermione dolls
creating bookmarks with potion bottles
and broomsticks
and owls on them
reading and re-reading the novels
renting and re-renting the movies from the library
sleeping in your Gryffindor nightie
and planning a Ginny Weasley costume

But then I catch myself
while washing dishes
or driving the car
wondering about this character or that
as though they were friends of mine
the wealthy businesswoman
contemplating her life's work
and the splitting of her business empire
the adolescent in a dystopian world
struggling to keep his body in one piece
as he flees demented authorities
the Dominican teenage poet
clinging to the written word
and discovering who she is

The magic of fiction
takes us into places we would never go
introduces us to people we would never meet
broadens our world with experiences we will never have
makes us more human
and suddenly your obsession with the boy who lived
makes perfect sense

Nostalgia of Now

Sometimes our life is like a montage
images of our children
being born
running through sprinklers
faces painted for Halloween
spinning in tutus or Easter dresses
and I can remember
anticipating these days
for years
but the montage runs faster and faster
and even as the days feel so long
full of squabbles, tantrums, and accidents
time speeds up
the monthly pages of the calendar fly into the wind
the ticker of the year spins
relentless
new shoes
bigger clothes
roll after roll of duct tape
box after box of Pull-Ups
bottles of acrylic paint and
bags of hot glue sticks—

How do we measure our life together
how do we honor their growth
and our own
the sweet pain of time passing
and nostalgia for the moments
that are happening before our eyes

Surprise

A glob of purple-pink
toothpaste
leisurely making its way
down the bathroom wall
in the hour
since my children
have brushed their teeth

A nebulous smell in the living room
which, upon searching,
is found to emanate
from a dried cat turd
nestled on the couch

A hairball in our bedroom
with accompanying cat cereal detritus
soaking through three layers of bed linens
yellow puddled
by my husband's pillow

But.

two sticky hands spontaneously grabbing my face

accompanied by "I love you, Mommy!"

graham cracker, honey, and peanut butter

formed into "cake pops" for my birthday

a quick shuffle and kick (in the right direction!)

at the Saturday soccer game

Gifts from the universe,

unexpected everyday reminders

of how we participate

in the dance between

what it is we think we want

and what is–

spinning,

flipping,

twirling upside down

and always,

being surprised.

Saturday Symphony

Our Saturday symphony begins
with the creak of a door
and a pause
then rushed slaps of sock feet
and rustles of covers
as my youngest
scrambles up
and snuggles with me in the bed

the whir of the coffee grinder

a chorus of breakfast requests
complaints about someone's
coughing in the night
or someone's wanting
new slippers

taps of silverware on dishes
scraping and sawing

a visit to the school community garden
and the discovery of beetles therein
yields squeals of delight
from some of our number
and horror from others of us
I confess to being part of the latter group

the buzz of my husband's band saw
and belt sander as he polishes a
new cutting board

huffs, purrs, and light snores
of an afternoon nap
marry with light strains
of a college football game

I am working out the chords to a
new song on my mandolin

laughing at the dinner table
someone wants to play a guessing game
the benches get pushed back
and stools pulled over to get a treat
from the top of the cabinet
then, running down the hall
to brush teeth
to say good night
to climb up bunk bed stairs
and settle in to sleep

the house, quiet, breathes relief
echoes of transcendent joy still
bouncing off the walls
we silently read, sew, sand a spoon
readying ourselves
for another day

Collective Memory

You are grinning up at me
in a unicorn pajama onesie
eyes fluttering
gap tooth smile

You are galloping in circles on the trampoline
in superhero underwear
and cowboy boots

You have red marks around your eyes
from wearing goggles
and are sporting a rainbow speckled swimsuit

Your face is yellowish green,
with lion whiskers and ears
the yellow paint having smudged with the black

You are putting together Russian nesting dolls
breathing heavily, immersed in your task,
heads and bottoms strewn across the table

You are strumming the major chord
which I have tuned on the kiddie guitar
with superficial frets
but what did we expect for $30

You are running from one corner of the house
to the other, in fringed boots
clutching your stuffed Darth Vader doll
singing Barbie songs
saving all of us from the bad guys

You are creating stories and relationships
between cake toppers
repurposed from birthday parties of years past:
Trolls, *Frozen*, *Lion King*

You have set up a magic fortress
in our backyard using a 3-man tent
which now smells like a feral cat hotel
from being unzipped for weeks
and has holes in the sides
from where pictures of Hermione
have been pinned
and to step in there
is to enter a workshop of
freedom, creativity, and ingenuity

You are creating your world
using duct tape, hot glue, and
recycled yogurt containers,
disappearing into the flow
of timelessness
which all artists know

The three of you are watching *Harry Potter*
reading books on the couch
playing cafe with wooden ice cream cones
splashing in our backyard kiddie pool
and the silence is a balm
before the bickering erupts
as it must
in the cycle of our days

Which are full:
synapses
ideas
jokes
lessons
ruptures
repairs
mistakes
traditions
laying a foundation
forming a collective memory
that will outlive all of us.

Hands

My hands are buried in pumpkin pulp
my fingers working to separate the seeds
and my mind wanders:
what if they were more skilled
what if they were in someone's chest,
working to mend a heart
or repair a bone

But oh, what pride!
In the scheme of human existence
on the timeline of life
and in the scale of the universe
are my hands not doing
exactly the magic they were made for

Feeling my son's forehead for a fever
repeating "Twinkle, Twinkle Little Star"
on my violin so that my daughter may learn
filling in the bubbles on a ballot
writing a card of gratitude to a friend
exploring the broad surface of my lover's chest
kneading bread for our dinner

In what economy
is that not enough?

Catch It If You Can

My days require so much mental energy and flexibility;
every day feels like training for a patience marathon,
like my expectations are pretzels that must be twisted
and looped back onto themselves

I have felt creative ideas come in a moment and fly away
just as quickly,
like some sort of butterfly that remains just out of reach

And my net is just too short, and just too slow

These days are like
getting caught in a spiderweb

Are your pants clean?
You have to *tell* us when you have to potty!

moving through Jell-O

Come here, it's time for dinner.
Come on, everyone is there.
There won't be a treat after dinner unless you come now.
No treat? Okay, that's fine.
Oh, you do want a treat? Well come on!

running against the wind with a parachute

Honey, I know, I saw.
I'm sorry he smacked you.
And I'm sorry you smacked him.
I know you didn't mean to.

changing a tire on a moving vehicle

Darling, I think these are pants where the boots go on
the outside.
I know, that's sad.
It makes me sad, too.

wearing your heart outside your body

God, I love you.

You Know

You know that sometimes
I shout too loudly
I snap too sharply
I speak too harshly

You know that sometimes
I sigh too heavily
I slump too deeply
I shuffle too wearily

You know that sometimes
you push my buttons
you humble me
you bring me to my knees
in frustration
exasperation
and helplessness

But do you know that
you hold up a mirror
reflecting all my insecurities
my impatience
my imperfections

Do you know that
when I look at you
I see myself
but alchemized
into something
someone
so free
so uninhibited
so brilliant
so beautiful

Do you know that
my dearest hope
is to welcome you
to adulthood
with all of that
still intact
and that hope
is heavy

Do you know that
when I hold you close
as I have since you were a baby
I still close my eyes
and breathe in the smell
of your hair

Do you know that
loving you
has made me
and is making me
who I am

Truths

Being your mother
is to know these truths:
You are sacred, precious, and holy
there is a spark of the divine in you
you are made of my blood
and that of my favorite human
you are composed of stardust and magic
woven together in my womb
and your body houses a soul
that is quite possibly older than my own

and also
why
why why
can you not act like
we are ever trying to get somewhere on time

Someday

I am old enough to know
that someday never comes
still, I stop
and realize

we have two independent readers
potty accidents have grown rare
everyone can sleep through the night
can pick out their own clothes
can reach their own snacks
can buckle themselves
I have mindspace and bandwidth
to think about something beyond
the weekly meal plan
or after school activities:
reading novels
writing poetry
playing music with no one attached to me
discovering who I am now
after three early childhoods

and I know that there may be
cars and boys and braces,
graduations, colleges, and apartments
in our distant future
but someday feels closer
than it used to.

Riding Currents

Poems write themselves
when I am not looking

as I sleep
my mind
takes the pieces
and tries them on
to see how they fit

simmers them
in a subconscious stew
melding words
into new flavors

and all I can do
is notice
how a conversation
uncovers my soul
before I can think
what I am saying

Birds of paradise
are blooming
without any help from me
and our children
are outgrowing clothes
and shoes
weekly

We blossom and unfold
learning our beauty
growing into our wings
and the best I can hope for
is to ride the currents
as they carry us
from here
to there.

Mother

Please know
that whatever decisions
I make about
the ways I speak to you
the ways I care for you
the ways I discipline you
are often motivated
by those things
my own mother
did right
or wrong
the way I saw it

I tell you this
so that when you are grown
you may have gentleness
when you look upon me
and so you are aware
when your own children
begin to individuate
from you
and call your actions
into question
and examine
your motives
you will know
this is a cycle
which runs
generation
to generation
to generation
world without end

and I hope
you will see this poem
as my gift to you
as a companion
on this journey.

Orbits

To have children
is to break your heart
into pieces
and to move through life
in the awareness
that those pieces
are on their own orbits
skinning their knees
having spats with friends
and mending them
or not
learning to play goalie
and to do multiplication
and write essays

at first your pathways
are along similar lines
sometimes exactly the same
sometimes more alike than
you wish they were

but time passes
and trajectories grow wider
and wilder
life dictates
unexpected ellipses
and ventures
into unexplored territory

but you
with your broken heart
are always aware
of where they began

Flag

On my walk I noticed
on a neighbor's door
the flag of Ukraine,
the top half cerulean blue,
the bottom half sunflower,
signifying a beautiful homeland–
I wonder what my flag would be

Would it be Carolina blue and russet clay,
rich, deep brown of the earth,
violet and saffron pansies,
lavender dianthus, raspberry azaleas,
periwinkle hydrangea, lilac rhododendron, or maybe
the cornsilk yellow and forest green of my childhood home,
mauve hugs from my mother

Would it be clear blue sky and
shades of beige, taupe, and cinnamon
of a rocky desert landscape
jade greens of saguaro, barrel, and fish hook cactus,
fuchsia and canary of cactus and prickly pear blossoms,
verdant bark and lemon bright blooms of Palo Verde,
magenta of bougainvillea, and
creamy white oleander,
sweet jasmine or orange blossom

Maybe it would be honey wheat hair and azure eyes,
pink palms,
summer-browned feet, and
watermelon-stained faces
or coffee brown eyes,
umber hair and beard
with grey strands that used to shine auburn in the sun.

These are my flag,
and I am home.

I'll Be Seeing You

It will be a car accident
a bike wreck
a tornado
a mass shooter
cancer
drowning
robbery

it will be an eating disorder
abuse
disease
a fall
an animal attack
a house fire
an earthquake

it will be childbirth
a murder
a rock slide
a plane crash
a wildfire
a flood

it will be suicide

I will say them all,
all the horrible things
then they will not happen
they can't–because
I will have imagined them
and death wants to catch us by surprise

My broken heart
my addled mind
my ragged soul
know this is not true

But I will prepare your vegetables
I will smother you with sunscreen
I will fasten your carseat
and make you wear your seatbelt
and teach you about guns
and keep the car maintained
and review your lockdown drill at school
and take you to the doctor

I will read books to you
and display your artwork all over the house
and spoon your body in mine
and braid your hair
and teach you all of the things I know
and take you to all of the places I have been
and have wanted to go
and do my best to show you the way
I will love you
fiercely and unwaveringly

And I will write
I will write what I want to tell you
but can't
I will write what you say
what you do
how it is to be your mother
and you will live forever
and I will live forever
and when our bodies die
they will melt into the earth
and evaporate into the sky
and our souls will meet again
on some heavenly plane
or in another life
in a jungle
on a mountain
in a distant city
on a cruise ship

And I will recognize your smile
I will know your hairline
I will know the shade of your eyes
and I won't remember what happened
in our last life together
or in any of them
I will just know that I know you
and have known you for a while
and am so glad to see you again.

Alive

You can break my music into
scales,
arpeggios,
and inversions
But you will not trace the magic,
You will not know why it marries with other voices in
irreplicable harmony,
Why it hides in the strumming of the guitar,
shining bright when it chooses,
dancing and flitting in and out of other melodies
And why I can't remember the notes I have played
With my eyes closed

If you cut open my chest you may find
bronchioles,
lungs,
and alveoli
But you will not see the life,
the air which fuels my brain and my body,
Which quickens as breath
when my son stumbles
on the concrete or
When my daughter says aloud
what I was just thinking
You may discover
milk ducts, glands, and lobes
within my breasts
But you won't measure the rush of love
and the feeling of home upon latching a baby
or why it still happens, the three thousandth time

You may draw my blood
and divide it into
red blood cells,
white blood cells,
and platelets
But you will not find there the feeling of its rush to my face,
to my fingers, to my toes, to my unseen parts
at the thought of my lover
The microscope will not reveal
the quivering I feel at his touch
or the shudders of painful pleasure

How much of us is stardust,
and how old is the blood in our veins?
How we long to hold the mystery in our hands
when its vast expanse fills the universe

Blue Ridge

Climbing the steep terrain of boulders
and a suggestion of gravel path
we reach the rise of the slope,
viewing the valley full of riotous wildflowers
royal, cornflower, scarlet, magenta, marigold
thrilling our eyes and healing our souls
enfolding us in nature's blanket of beauty

We hear the waterfall before we see it,
rushing and swirling over the rocks
gathering in a cool, clear pool
and inviting us to step into the fresh stream alongside
soothing our aching feet–
the breeze dances on our wet skin,
peace at the end of the journey.

Streaks of cerulean, lavender, fiery pink expand
across the sky
gossamer wisps stretching and fading with the setting sun
we sit on the hill as rays from the warm yellow orb
grow softer and softer
and our conversation grows sparse
with the delicate web of light

Impulse

Twirling to Swan Lake
in the front room of my childhood home,
my 8-year-old frame lithe and slight,
movements untrained, hardly fluid
but feeling the music.
My father sits
nodding appreciatively and dozing gently
at the end of his workday.
Free and unencumbered,
my body moves by impulse.

Stroking our cat as she nurses kittens
she birthed in the floorboard of our open Jeep
her 6-toed paws stretch and curl in satisfaction
as tiny mouths work on tiny nipples
and she dozes
knowing there is not a damn thing
she should be doing instead.
Free and unencumbered,
her body moves by impulse.

Groaning and squatting
as my husband massages my hips
I envision myself opening
and my baby emerging,
I breathe fully into my belly
and ride the surges with
deep roars, knowing ancestral power.
Covered with blood and amnion,
the little one latches and suckles,
the motion of her mouth
having been practiced in the womb.
Free and unencumbered,
our bodies move by impulse.

Waiting

In this world of Amazon Prime
and blueberries in winter,
what does it mean to wait?

What does it feel like
to let it soak,
to let it grow,
to leave it to develop
on its own

rather than reading another book
about sleep training
or churning out
another 500 uninspired words
or signing up
for another business webinar?

How is it to take a chance
on trusting the rhythms of the seasons—
facing lean times with courage
knowing that the wheel
will turn again soon enough,
and that future blessings may be diminished
by scrabbling for them now?

Anyone who has eaten
a store-bought peach knows.

Timing is everything.

Offering

My daughter tenderly digs
a pocket
in the granite sand–
down
into the soft black
and places the quartz
(and a few dried petals)
in the cool wash
her sister reverently covers the hole
little brother gathers branches
and the three of them
place twigs, rocks, and bark
carefully on top of the parcel

I feel the earth purring
in appreciation of our gratitude
vibrating with our energy
welcoming our honor
reveling in our wonder
and I feel alive, too

Stardust

"we are stardust"
she breathes
her voice heavy with reverence
"the same thing that's in stars–
    it's in us"
she enunciates, eyes wide
instructing her sister and brother
in the mystery
  the beauty
  the magic
of where humanity
grazes the divine

Muse

Sometimes the Muse comes
in the light of a full moon
during a candlelit bath
or while meditating in a silk robe
or while reading some rare, esoteric wisdom and
        sipping fine tea

Then again, sometimes Sleep cruelly
elbows her out of the way
and you fall asleep three different times
during the two hours before bedtime

The Muse doesn't wait until
everyone is potty trained
or until everyone can brush their own hair
brush their own teeth
dress themselves
remember their shoes
and their bags
and their books
or until everyone knows how to
stay in their damn beds
after bedtime

She doesn't wait until
all the dishes are done
the floors are clean
the clothes are folded
all the clutter is tidied

But she will sneak in
while you chop onions
or wipe bottoms
or braid hair
while you drive to school, or
perhaps on the way back home
in silence
or in a car full of singing and screaming

She will tap your shoulder as you lie in bed
those first or last five minutes of the day
that you are conscious
or while you are nursing,
feeling full and grateful
and wondering how it will all get done again
tomorrow

Drops

I
love
how
water
drops
break
through
rocks
just
by
staying
steady
and
doing
the
damn
thing

Turning

Our home is a spinning orb
dancing through space
rotating in harmony with moon, stars, and planets

I see the spheres reflected
in the pupils of my children's eyes,
in the bowls of the pottery market,
the mustard and white tile of our kitchen backsplash

Heavy globes of grapefruit and oranges droop on branches
of the trees in our neighborhood
blossoms open full,
wound woods closing

Circles of life:
the moon and her pull on the tides
my breasts, replete with sustaining milk
my once-swollen womb, stretched from the work of three
pregnancies

Ever expanding, ever contracting
ever returning, yet ever exploring
our world turns
and keeps turning

Dance

I find my space in the cosmos
as half of a dyad
birthing creation
a poppy seed
swirling life inside me
made of stardust, both of us

I welcome my lover
in a rhythmic embrace
as the fetus inside me turns and floats
rolling in my internal ocean
and my muscles surge
thrusting him into the light
from the cold, the wet, the dark

my infant pulls my nipple
far into his mouth and,
having sent cells of his own
spinning into my blood,
my heart, my brain
he hungrily gulps my body
poured out for him

we intertwine
and we separate
orbiting each other
in seasons
as humans have done
since the beginning of humans
and will do

until we all die away
our dance fading
into eternity
a memory in the earth

If I Were God

If I were God
I would want you
to pet the cat
to lay your head
on her soft fur
feel her body purring
scratch her ears
be charmed as she lifts her chin
and smooth it with your finger
feel her paw in your hand
and adore her

I would want you
to hold your children
to cradle them
however small or big they are
to run your fingers through their hair
to bury your face by their scalp
and smell the sweet fragrance
of clean sweat
that has always intoxicated you
to welcome them
however dirty
however angry
however sad
into your arms
and into your spirit

I would want you
to enjoy your lover

to feel their firm, supple flesh
under your hand
to smell their earthy aroma
to discover their hidden places
to taste pleasure
and to see yourself
reflected in their eyes

I would want you to know
that the universe
is so big
and you
are so small
and no one needs
for you to know everything
about anything

In Time

When I flounder
my subconscious reassures me
that it is okay to question
that I don't have to know all the answers
and that it might take some time
–a lifetime–
to figure it out

What does it mean?
How are these connected?
What is happening here?

It takes effort to wonder
it takes thought to examine
but I have it
I have the energy
I have the resources
I have the space
to find the way
in time

Wings

I learn
I grow
I fall
I expand
I bend
I stretch
I fail
I flow
I fly
I change
my mind
I take up
every inch
of my space
I breathe
every molecule
of my air
I do not apologize
for my expansiveness
Because the universe
can hold all of me
And the world
needs
my depth
and breadth
And I am not afraid

My Catechism

What should we do?
Who should we be?

We are already doing it
We are inhaling
exhaling
feeling
loving
smiling
caressing
creating
singing
twirling
eating
sleeping
learning
falling
bleeding
trying
growing
trusting

How can we earn
the air we breathe
the space we take up?

We can never earn these things
and yet,
we already have

God

God crackles in electric air before the storm
smelling of ozone
rising in waves of heat from the pavement
rumbling as distant thunder

God unfurls as a jasmine vine
tendrils climbing, ever reaching
both the sun, and the leaves
and the glucose creating energy

God lands on an organ pipe
bobbing and popping bright red
God is a chirp
a trill
a whir
and God blooms bright yellow
fuchsia
rich orange
among knobbly arms of pale green cactus

God is two zygotes
and their joining in warm, wet womb
the slow gestation
the quickening of movement
the sudden and final surge
out of saline water
and into the bracing air
both of which
God is
growth into willowy adolescent
whose tiny face I still have memorized

God is the learning
the un-learning
the re-learning
the dance
the labyrinth
seen, unseen
and everything between

this I know
for all creation tells me so

9 781956 604115